W9-CGS-280

Religions of the World

Buddhism

Anita Ganeri

Please visit our web site at: www.worldalmanaclibrary.com
For a free color catalog describing World Almanac® Library's list of high-quality books and multimedia programs, call 1-800-848-2928 (USA) or 1-800-387-3178 (Canada). World Almanac® Library's fax: (414) 332-3567.

Library of Congress Cataloging-in-Publication Data

Ganeri, Anita, 1961–
Buddhism / by Anita Ganeri.
p. cm. — (Religions of the world)
Includes bibliographical references and index.
ISBN 0-8368-5865-4 (lib. bdg.)
ISBN 0-8368-5871-9 (softcover)
1. Buddhism—Juvenile literature. I. Title.
II. Religions of the world (Milwaukee, Wis.)
BQ4032.G35 2005
294.3—dc22 2005041708

This edition first published in 2006 by
World Almanac® Library
330 West Olive Street, Suite 100
Milwaukee, WI 53212 USA

Subject consultant: The Clear Vision Trust
Project Editor, Hodder Wayland: Kirsty Hamilton
Editor: Nicola Barber
Designer: Janet McCallum
Picture Researcher: Shelley Noronha, Glass Onion Pictures
Maps and artwork: Peter Bull
World Almanac® Library editor: Gini Holland
World Almanac® Library cover design: Kami Koenig

Photo Credits
The publisher would like to thank the following for permission to reproduce their pictures:
Bridgeman Art Library www.bridgeman.co.uk/Ashmolean Museum/University of Oxford 6, National Museum of India, New Delhi, India 18, 24; CIRCA Photo Library/William Holtby 16, 22, 44; Clear Vision Trust 43; Corbis/Keren Su 29; Exile Images/N. Cooper 25, H. Davies 40; Robert Harding Picture Library 4, J. Sweeney 10, A. Woolfitt 13, D. Traverso 15, G. Hellier 28, D. Beatty 34, A. Woolfitt 35, U. Gahwiler 37; Hutchison Picture Library 7, 19, 20, 33, 41; Ann and Bury Peerless 8, 9, 11, 17, 38, 39; © M. L. Sinibaldi/Corbis: cover; Topfoto 21, 31, 36, 42, 45; ZUL 23, 27, 30, 32

Printed in China

1 2 3 4 5 6 7 8 9 09 08 07 06 05

Contents

Note

There are often two spellings for the key terms in Buddhism, depending on whether they are written in Pali or Sanskrit, two ancient languages of India. For example, the Pali word for the Buddha's teaching is Dhamma; *the Sanskrit is* Dharma. *Throughout this book, the most commonly known spelling is used. Dates are written using* B.C.E. *("Before Common Era") and* C.E. *("Common Era") instead of* B.C. *(Before Christ) and* A.D. *(Anno Domini, which is Latin for "in the year of our Lord"). The dates are the same in both systems.*

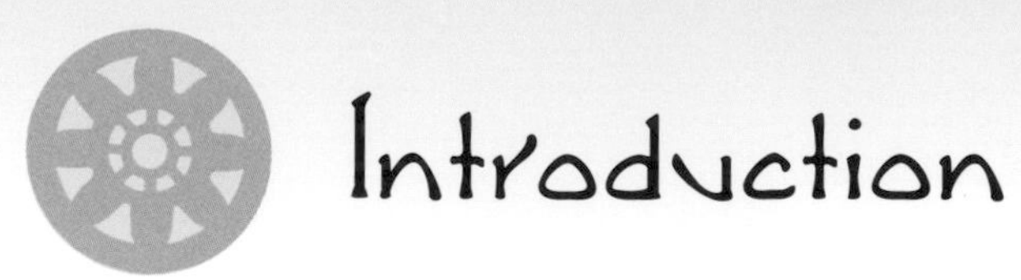

Introduction

Buddhism is one of the world's major religions. It began in northern India about 2,500 years ago when a royal prince, Siddhartha Gautama, first taught people a way to free themselves from suffering. He became known as the Buddha, the Enlightened One, or "the One who knows the Truth." Buddhists use his teachings, which they call the Dharma, as a guide for their lives and as a path to an understanding of the way life is. (A more detailed account of the Buddha's life is described in the next chapter.)

The Buddhist World

By the time of the Buddha's death, thousands of people in India had become his followers. Like him, many gave up their homes and possessions and became monks and nuns. They travelled around the country, teaching the Dharma. From India, Buddhism spread all over Asia. In each country, it adapted to local customs and often mingled with local beliefs. Today, there are an estimated four hundred million Buddhists. The population of some countries, such as Thailand, is mostly Buddhist. In other countries, Buddhists form the minority. More recently, Buddhism has become increasingly popular in Europe, North America, and Australia.

➤ *Buddhists honor the Buddha by bowing and making offerings to an image of the Buddha, as this monk in Sri Lanka is doing.*

The Buddha's Teaching

Buddhism is unusual among the world's religions, because it is not based on belief in a divine being, called God, who created the world and watches over it. The Buddha did not claim to be a god and did not expect to be worshiped as one. Rather, he was a human being who gained Enlightenment and understood the truth about life and how human beings can come to understand it. Through his teaching, people had the chance to achieve Enlightenment for themselves. The Buddha, however, urged all his followers not to accept his teachings blindly, but to test them against their own experience.

Modern Developments

Over the last two hundred years, Buddhism has faced many challenges, from social to political and economic. In some parts of the world, materialism has weakened its influence. In others, Buddhists have been persecuted under harsh political regimes. Yet despite these challenges, Buddhist practices such as meditation are becoming a part of many people's everyday lives. So what does the future hold for Buddhism? A key Buddhist teaching states that everything is always changing. Nothing stays the same. It remains to be seen how Buddhism will deal with the changes it faces in the twenty-first century.

A map showing the estimated number of Buddhists in countries around the world today. Note: Some countries such as Tibet have relatively small populations but their religion is predominantly Buddhist.

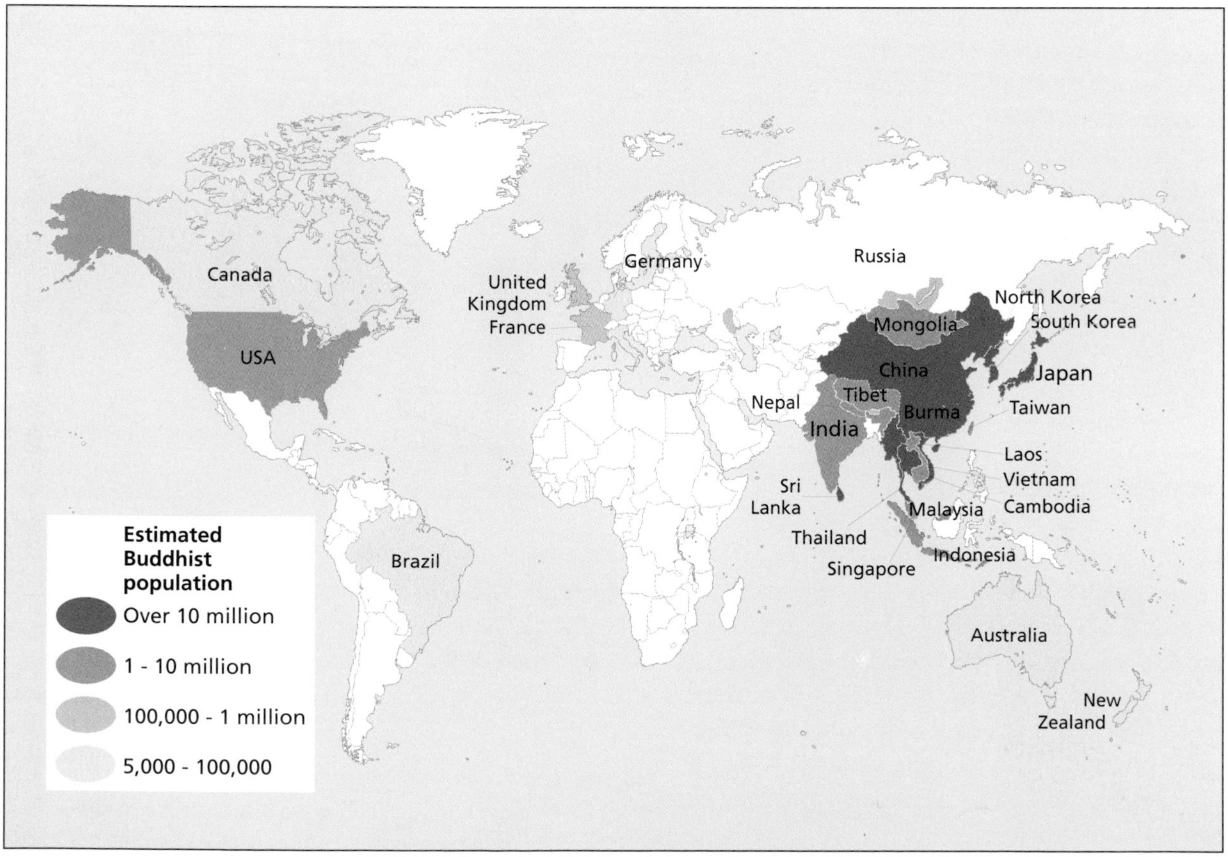

History of Buddhism

According to tradition, Siddhartha Gautama was born in about 563 B.C.E. in Lumbini, in present-day Nepal. Our knowledge of Siddhartha comes partly from early sacred texts and partly from later commentaries. Many legends also grew up around his life. These were recorded centuries after his death and may not be historically accurate.

Birth of the Buddha

According to the legends, Siddhartha was the son of King Suddodhana, the leader of the Shakya clan who lived in northeast India, on the border with Nepal. His mother was Queen Maya. One night, legend says, Queen Maya dreamed that she was visited by a white elephant—a sign that she would have a baby who would grow into an exceptional person. Siddhartha was born on the full moon of May in a beautiful garden in Lumbini, Nepal.

Seven days later, Siddhartha's mother died, so Siddhartha was brought up by his aunt in his father's luxurious palace. Here he was visited by an old wise man, called Asita, who foretold his future. Asita told the king that his son would grow up to be either a great ruler or a great teacher, depending on whether or not he ever stopped to think about suffering. Determined that Siddhartha should become a great ruler, the king tried to keep all knowledge of suffering from him. He kept him safe in the palace, surrounded by fine things. Guards were set around the palace to prevent him from seeing the outside world.

This stone carving shows the birth of the Buddha. It dates from the second or third centuries C.E.

As part of his upbringing, Siddhartha was taught the warrior skills he would need as a prince. At sixteen years old, he was married to a princess, Yasodhara, from a neighboring kingdom, with whom he had a son, Rahula.

A tree festooned with prayer flags in the sacred garden in Lumbini, Nepal, where the Buddha is said to have been born. Written on the flags are Buddhist prayers that blow to all corners of the earth.

Religion in India

The sixth century B.C.E.*, when Siddhartha was born, was a time of great religious change in India. Old ideas were being challenged and new ideas formulated. The main religion of India then was a form of Hinduism (as it still is today). It is thought that Siddhartha may have been brought up as a Hindu, although no one knows for certain. As the Buddha, Siddhartha strongly criticized the Hindu priests who came from the Brahmin (upper) caste. They were seen as religious authorities and were very powerful. The Buddha taught that it was how people behaved, rather than the class into which they were born, that really mattered. According to the Buddha, the path to Enlightenment was open to everyone, whether rich or poor, high or low caste.*

The Four Sights

Siddhartha lived very comfortably in his father's palace. Then, when he was twenty-nine years old, he had an experience that changed his life. Disobeying his father's orders, he ordered his charioteer, Channa, to take him for a ride outside the palace walls. He was horrified by the grief and suffering he saw around him: a hunched old man, a sick man in great pain, and a corpse in a funeral procession. Channa explained that this was a normal part of life. Every day, people grew old, fell ill, and died. Then Siddhartha saw a holy man, dressed in a worn robe, who had given up his home and possessions to search for a way to true happiness. He had nothing, but he looked deeply content.

That night, Siddhartha returned to the palace, his mind made up. He would leave his luxurious life behind and follow the example of the holy man. Secretly, he said goodbye to his wife and baby son and left the palace. After riding all night, he came to the banks of a river where he cut off his long, black hair and exchanged his fine clothes for a simple robe. From now on, he would live as a wandering holy man with no money, belongings, or home.

▼ *This wall-painting from Thailand shows the Four Sights that Siddhartha saw on his chariot ride. They revealed to him that people suffered, grew old, and died as a normal part of life. On the right is the last of the Four Sights, the holy man.*

The Search for Enlightenment

Siddhartha joined two religious teachers and learned how to meditate. Next, he spent six years in the forest with five other holy men. There Siddhartha lived a life of great hardship, believing that this would help him to become wiser. He wore rags, went for months on end without washing, spent long periods without moving, pulled out his hair and beard, and slept on a bed of thorns. None of these practices helped him in his search for the truth. Finally, weak and exhausted, he left his companions and made his way to a village that is now known as Bodh Gaya. That evening, he sat under a tall bodhi tree and began to meditate.

During the night, legend says, Siddhartha was visited by Mara, the evil one, who tried to tempt him away from his search for the truth. Siddhartha ignored the temptation, continued to meditate, and Mara fled. As the night drew on, Siddhartha finally found the answers he had been looking for. Suddenly, he saw the truth about why people suffered and how he could help them. He now became the Buddha, the Enlightened, or awakened, One.

➤ *An image from a temple in Vietnam of Siddhartha meditating under the bodhi tree. Many Buddhists temples and* viharas *(temples or monasteries) have statues like this one to remind people of the story of the Buddha's Enlightenment.*

The First Teaching

After his Enlightenment, the Buddha continued to meditate for many more days and nights. He was filled with a great sense of peace and happiness. During this time, he received his first two followers. These were two passing merchants who gave him food. Determined to teach other people what he had discovered, the Buddha made his way to the Deer Park at Sarnath where he found the five holy men who had been his companions in the forest (*see page* 9). To them he gave his first teaching, in which he explained the cause of suffering (*see page 16*). His words were so convincing and powerful that the holy men quickly gained Enlightenment. They then formally pledged to follow the Buddha and his teachings.

Traveling and Teaching

For the next forty-five years, the Buddha traveled around northeast India teaching people from all walks of life. His followers—monks, nuns, and laypeople—became known as the *Sangha*, or Buddhist community.

▼ *The Dhamekh Stupa in Sarnath, India, is said to stand on the very spot where the Buddha gave his first teaching after his Enlightenment. This stupa is an important place of pilgrimage for Buddhists.*

This carved stone statue from Sri Lanka shows the Buddha's *parinirvana*. Legend says that when he passed away, the Buddha lay on his right-hand side and that an earthquake shook the earth.

During this time, the Buddha helped many other people achieve Enlightenment. They became known as *arahats*, or "worthy ones," and were sent out by the Buddha to teach. The year after his Enlightenment, the Buddha returned home to visit his family. He was reconciled with his father, who became an arahat, and his aunt, who became the first nun. He also ordained his young son, Rahula, as a monk.

Passing Away

When the Buddha was about eighty years old, he fell ill with food poisoning and knew that his life was drawing to an end. He told his faithful companion, Ananda, not to look for another leader when he was gone but to let the Dharma be a guide for his followers. Then he called the monks together and made his last journey to the village of Kushinagara. Just outside the town, he stopped in a grove of trees where he lay down to rest. His last words were to remind the monks of the teaching that everything changes and passes away. Then he died. This event is known as the *parinirvana*, which means the final extinction of greed, hatred, and ignorance.

After the Buddha's death, the monks held a ceremony in his honor that lasted for six days. Then his body was cremated. His ashes were divided into eight parts and given to the rulers of eight different clans. Dome-shaped burial monuments, called *stupas*, were built over them (*see page 28*).

Buddhism Splits

During the Buddha's life, his teachings were not written down. Instead, they were memorized by his followers and passed on by word of mouth. Shortly after his death, it is said, a council of monks was called to collect all the teachings together. Nothing, however, was written down until several centuries later. Soon, different opinions began to arise among the various groups of monks about what the Buddha had actually taught. These disagreements became stronger at a second council, held about fifty to one hundred years after the Buddha's death. The main disagreement was over the rules about how monks and nuns should live. Subsequently, Buddhism split into two groups—*Theravada*, or "the way of the elders," and *Mahayana*, or "the great way" (*see page 18*).

Buddhism Spreads

Despite the split between the two groups, Buddhism continued to spread very quickly in India and throughout the rest of Asia. Theravada Buddhism spread south and east to Sri Lanka, Myanmar (Burma), Cambodia, Laos, and Thailand. It reached Sri Lanka in about 250 B.C.E., when the son of Emperor

This map shows how the two main schools of Buddhism—Mayahana and Theravada—disseminated out of India and became established in other countries around the world.

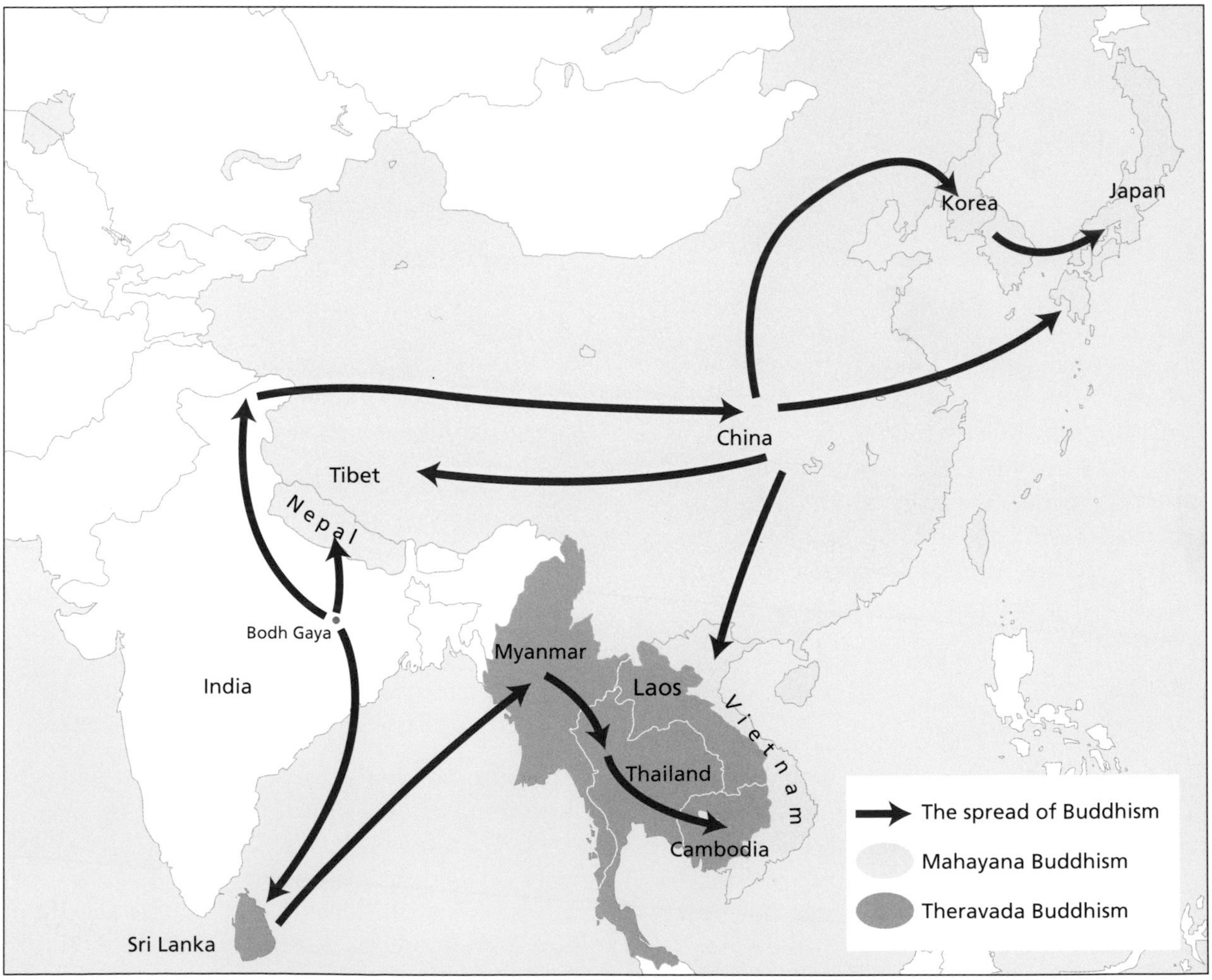

Ashoka (*see box*) converted the king and most of the islanders. Mahayana Buddhism spread north and west to Nepal, Tibet, China, Japan, Vietnam, and Korea. Buddhism first reached China in the first century C.E., along the trade route known as the Silk Road. By the twelfth century C.E., however, Buddhism had almost disappeared from India, its original home. Two factors may have caused its decline—its merger with local religions, and the fact that its peaceful nature made it vulnerable to the military might of invaders, such as the Muslim Mogul rulers of northern India, who were of Mongol, Turkish, and Persian origins.

Emperor Ashoka

The great Indian emperor, Ashoka Maurya, came to the throne in 268 B.C.E. Through a series of military campaigns, he quickly expanded his empire to include most of India, apart from the southern tip. After one particularly bloody battle, in which one hundred thousand people were killed, Ashoka was filled with remorse for the suffering his greed had caused. He vowed to set up a society based not on violence but on the Buddhist principles of peace and compassion. All over his empire, he erected pillars on which decrees were carved, telling people to live just, truthful, and generous lives. Ashoka himself tried to set an example. He established hospitals for the poor and built wells and reservoirs. He also sent missionaries, including his own son and daughter, far and wide to spread the Buddha's teachings.

➤ *The famous lion capital (top) from Ashoka's pillar in Sarnath, India. The four back-to-back lions were Ashoka's symbols and represented bravery. They are now the state symbol of modern India.*

Beliefs and Sacred Texts

Despite differences in how they interpret the Buddha's teachings and practice their faith, the different groups of Buddhists share the same basic beliefs. For example, Buddhists believe that when a person dies, he or she is born again in a different form—a human body, a plant, or an animal. This is also called reincarnation, a belief Buddhists share with Hindus. The Buddha's teachings are set down and explained in the Buddhist sacred texts. Unlike other religions, such as Islam and Christianity, Buddhism does not have just one main sacred text. Each group of Buddhists follows its own set of scriptures.

The Turning of the Wheel

In the first teaching he gave, to the five holy men, the Buddha explained that life was like a wheel in which everyone was caught, endlessly turning in a cycle of birth, death, and rebirth. What kept the wheel turning was *karma*—actions and their consequences. This meant that people's future happiness depended on the way they behaved. The only way to escape this endless cycle of birth and death was to move towards *nirvana*, or Enlightenment. By behaving kindly and wisely a person would move nearer to Enlightenment, while selfishness and unkindness would lead him or her further away from Enlightenment.

Three Marks of Being

Another crucial part of the Buddha's teachings is called the Three Marks of Being. These are *dukkha*, *anicca*, and *anatta*. Everything the Buddha taught is based on these three signs.

1. Dukkha is a Pali word that means "that which is difficult to bear." It can mean suffering physical illness, or pain, but it also includes feelings of boredom and frustration, and awareness of other people's suffering.

2. Anicca means "impermanence." Anicca means that everything is constantly changing and nothing lasts forever. Plants and animals die. Loved ones pass away. Even seemingly solid rocks and mountains slowly erode and crumble away.

3. Anatta means "no fixed self." Many religions believe a person has a soul or spirit which lives on after the death of the body. The Buddha taught that if we look at our own experience we will see that everything about us is always changing, including our emotions and thoughts. Therefore, there cannot be anything about us that is fixed or permanent, including our own self.

The Five Parts of a Person

The Buddha taught that human beings are made up of five parts, or elements, called *skandhas*. The word skandha means "bundle."

The five elements are: form (our physical bodies); sensation (our feelings); perception (our senses); determination (our thoughts); and consciousness (our awareness).

The way in which all five of these elements come together changes with each rebirth and is what makes everyone different.

This painting from Tibet shows Yama, the Lord of Death, holding the Wheel of Life. It represents the cycle of birth, death, and rebirth. Around the outside of the wheel are the different stages of a person's life. Inside are some of the various ways in which a person might be reborn. The three animals in the middle stand for confusion, greed, and hatred. These must be overcome in order to achieve Enlightenment.

The Four Noble Truths

In the second part of his teaching, the Buddha explained why people feel dissatisfied with their lives and how they can rise above this dissatisfaction to find happiness. This teaching is called the Four Noble Truths:

1. Everyone experiences dukkha, or suffering, in life.
2. Suffering is caused by people's greed, selfishness, and lack of contentment with what they have.
3. There is a way to end suffering.
4. The way to end suffering is to follow the Noble Eightfold Path.

The Noble Eightfold Path

In his life, the Buddha experienced both luxury and great hardship, and he knew that neither led to happiness. He taught the Noble Eightfold Path, a middle path for people to take between those two extremes. The Path shows eight ways in which people should live:

1. Right understanding—seeing through experience that the Buddha's teaching about life is true.
2. Right intention—having compassion for other people and thinking about people in a kind, generous way.
3. Right speech—not telling lies, swearing, or speaking harshly but using words that are helpful and kind. In some cases, it is better to stay silent if one cannot think of something useful to say.
4. Right action—treating other people well and not doing anything to harm them, such as killing or stealing.

This group of images in a temple in Myanmar shows the Buddha teaching the Four Noble Truths during his first teaching in the Deer Park in Sarnath.

5. Right livelihood—earning your living by doing something that helps the world and does not harm other people or animals.
6. Right effort—making an effort to do your best to be kind and avoid doing harm.
7. Right mindfulness—being calm and aware of your actions, feelings, and thoughts.
8. Right concentration—training your mind to be calm and peaceful through meditation.

Nirvana

Nirvana is the Buddhist term for the perfect peace and happiness entered when the circle of birth, death, and rebirth is broken, and all suffering ends. The word literally means "blown out." In a Buddhist story, a house is burning with three fires of hatred, greed, and ignorance, causing great unhappiness. Following the Dharma helps to blow the fires out. When all three fires are extinguished, suffering ends, and there is nirvana.

In Our Own Words

"Nirvana, or Enlightenment, is a way of experiencing life. If, one day, I become free from greed, hatred, and ignorance and can see things just as they are, I'll be positive whatever happens. I won't expect things to last, or to make me happy, so I won't suffer when they don't! As I am now, I may feel happy when I have cake in front of me, and a bit sad when it rains. But if I were Enlightened, my mood wouldn't depend on what was going on at the time, so I would be emotionally free. What a relief!"

The eight-spoked Dharma wheel is an important symbol in Buddhism. The spokes stand for the eight steps on the Noble Eightfold Path.

Theravada and Mahayana

All Buddhists follow the teachings of the Buddha, but they interpret and practice these teachings in different ways. Theravada Buddhists follow the Buddha and study the earliest scriptures in which his teachings are recorded. Mahayana Buddhists follow later Enlightened Buddhist teachers as well as the Buddha himself, and they have additional, later scriptures. They also worship heroic figures known as *bodhisattvas* (*see box below*).

Bodhisattvas

The word bodhisattva *means a "being of Enlightenment." According to Mahayana belief, a bodhisattva is a heroic figure who has gained Enlightenment and become a Buddha. Out of compassion, bodhisattvas choose to help other people to overcome suffering. Selflessly, they put the happiness of other beings in the world before their own, and people pray to them for help and guidance. There are thousands of bodhisattvas. One of the most popular is Avalokiteshvara, who represents perfect compassion. His name means "the Lord who looks down." He is often depicted with a thousand arms that show that he is ready to help everyone at once. He also has eleven heads and a thousand eyes to help him see all suffering beings. Mayahana Buddhists believe that we can all become more like bodhisattvas: full of kindness and concern for the world.*

➤ *This Tibetan painting shows the bodhisattva, Avalokiteshvara. He is worshiped, especially in Tibet, for his great compassion and care for those who are suffering.*

Zen Buddhism

One of the best-known branches of Mahayana Buddhism, Zen, is practiced mainly in Japan and China. It has also become popular in the West. According to tradition, an Indian monk called Bodhidharma introduced Zen into China in the fifth century C.E. The word *Zen* means "meditation" or "contemplation," and Zen Buddhists emphasize meditation as a way to experience the truth behind all things and see the world as it really is. Learning to meditate can take many years, but Zen Buddhists use different techniques to help them see life more clearly, including painting, writing poetry, gardening, and martial arts such as karate. These are all seen as ways of reaching directly into reality.

Tibetan Buddhism

Buddhism reached Tibet from India in the seventh century C.E. when the Tibetan king's two Buddhist wives encouraged him to convert. A long struggle followed between Buddhism and Bon, the ancient Tibetan religion. By the fourteenth century, however, Buddhism had become the country's main religion. Tibetan Buddhism is a mixture of Mahayana and Tantric beliefs, and it includes many colorful rites and rituals to help on the path to Enlightenment. (Tantric Buddhism is based on a set of texts that describe rituals, magic, and meditation techniques.) Many bodhisattvas are worshiped, including Avalokiteshvara. Today, Tibetan Buddhism faces an uncertain future, following the Chinese takeover of the country (*see page 43*).

▼ *A Zen monk, dressed in his traditional black robes, bows reverently in a monastery in Japan. Zen monks undergo very strict training in meditation.*

Buddhism in Daily Life

All Buddhists try to follow the example of the Buddha's life and to live by his teachings in everything they do. This means cultivating the qualities of wisdom, loving compassion, and morality. Buddhists believe that if they are kind, generous, truthful, helpful, and patient they will suffer less, cause less suffering, and help others suffer less. They also believe that people are naturally kind and wise, but because they don't understand the truth about life, they often behave unkindly. People think that things will make them happy, and they keep wanting things—trying to hold on to them and keep them the same. This makes people selfish and greedy. Buddhism, however, teaches its followers to accept that things are always changing. As people become kinder, wiser, and more contented with what they have got, they gradually move nearer to Enlightenment: perfect compassion and contentment with life as it is.

A monk meditates under a peepul tree in Lumbini, the birthplace of the Buddha. Buddhists try to follow the example of the Buddha in all aspects of their everyday lives.

The Three Jewels

In their daily lives, Buddhists commit themselves to the Three Jewels of Buddhism: the Buddha himself, as a great teacher and as the symbol of everyone's potential to gain Enlightenment; the Dharma, the Buddha's teaching; and the Sangha, the community of Buddhist laypeople, monks, and nuns. These are called jewels, or treasures, because they are so precious. Every day, Buddhists show that they place their trust in the Three Jewels by reciting these words:

> "I go for refuge to the Buddha
> I go for refuge to the Dharma
> I go for refuge to the Sangha."

The Five Moral Precepts

Buddhists also follow a set of guidelines, called the Five Moral Precepts. They undertake:

1. Not to kill or harm living beings.
2. Not to steal or take things that are not freely given.
3. To avoid sexual misconduct.
4. Not to speak unkindly or tell lies.
5. Not to drink alcohol or take drugs that might cloud the mind.

Each Precept also has a positive side. For example, it is not enough to avoid harming living beings. You should actively show kindness and compassion. The Five Positives are to develop loving-kindness, generosity, contentment, kindly and truthful speech, and mindfulness, or clear awareness.

A Japanese Buddhist prays for peace during a vigil in Union Square, New York, after the terrorist attacks of September 11, 2001.

In Our Own Words

"Every day, I try to remember that everything I do, think, and say has an effect on me and others. I meditate for about forty-five minutes before breakfast. It helps me notice how I am feeling. If I know I'm in a bad mood, I can be careful not to take it out on others. I try to speak kindly, even when disagreeing with someone, and I recycle or compost as much of my rubbish as possible so as to lessen my effect on our world. I love humor, and the thing I have had to work hardest at is not making insensitive and hurtful jokes. I can't be perfect, but I try my best, and apologize when I slip up."

Sacred Texts

Hundreds of sacred texts in Buddhism are linked to the various traditions and schools. Some texts contain the teachings of the Buddha; others are commentaries or writings by later Buddhist monks and teachers. Chanting from the sacred texts is an important part of Buddhist practice. Monks and nuns study the texts and help laypeople understand their meaning.

Collecting the Texts

For centuries after the Buddha's death, monks learned his teachings by heart and passed them on by word of mouth. Groups of monks met regularly to recite the teachings so that they did not forget them. In the first century B.C.E., as the numbers of monks fell, the teachings were finally written down in Pali, an ancient Indian language. These texts became the sacred texts of the Theravada Buddhists. Later texts were written down in Sanskrit, another ancient and sacred Indian language. Therefore, two spellings—the Pali and the Sanskrit—are often given for Buddhist words. For example, nirvana is the Sanskrit word; in Pali, it is *nibbana*. Most Buddhists prefer one language more than the other in their practice but are open to both.

▼ *This painting from Myanmar shows a scene from a Buddhist story called a* Jataka. *The* Jatakas *are part of the* Tipitaka *(see page 23) and tell the stories of the Buddha's past lives. In this story, "The Goodness of the Elephant King," the Buddha appears as an elephant to teach about generosity and gratitude.*

▲ *Some pages from a copy of the* Tipitaka. *The text is written in Pali on palm leaves, shaped into rectangular pages to copy the format that was used when the* Tipitaka *was first recorded.*

The Tipitaka

The sacred texts of the Theravada Buddhists are called the *Tipitaka*, which means "Three Baskets." This is because the texts were first written down on palm leaves, stored in three collections, or "baskets." The first "basket," the *Vinaya Pitaka*, sets out the rules laid down by the Buddha for how monks and nuns should live. The second "basket" is the *Sutta Pitaka*, which contains discourses by the Buddha on the key teachings of Buddhism. The third "basket," the *Abhi Dhamma Pitaka*, is made up of commentaries that help to explain the Buddha's teachings. The *Tipitaka* is also known as the *Pali Canon*. Most of the *Tipitaka*'s several thousand pages are now available in English.

The Metta Sutta

The Metta Sutta *is found in the* Sutta Pitaka, *the second basket of the* Tipitaka. *It is a famous discourse, or talk, given by the Buddha on the importance of* metta, *or loving-kindness. It is recited as part of everyday Buddhist practice by monks and laypeople. This is part of the* Metta Sutta:

"May all beings be well and happy,
may their hearts be whole and pure!
Whatever living beings there be—
Weak or strong, tall or short,
Small or large, seen or unseen,
Living far or near, those who are
Born and those yet to be born—
May all beings, without exception,
be happy!"

Mahayana Scriptures

Mahayana Buddhists have their own sacred texts, called *sutras*. Most of these texts were originally written down in Sanskrit from about the first century C.E. and were later translated into Chinese, Tibetan, and Japanese. For Mahayana Buddhists, some of these texts are believed to be the genuine word of the Buddha. Others were written by later Enlightened teachers; some have no author. They were considered so precious that, centuries ago, monks made long and dangerous journeys to obtain copies of them from India.

The Lotus Sutra

The *Lotus Sutra* is one of the most popular Mahayana texts, especially in Japan and China. This sutra is in the form of a talk given by the Buddha to a huge gathering of followers and bodhisattvas. In it, the Buddha puts forward the key Mahayana belief that everyone has the potential to gain Enlightenment. To explain this idea, the Buddha compares himself to a rain cloud that rains down on all plants, large and small. In the same way, the Buddha "rains down" the Dharma, and everyone may benefit in his or her own way.

This illustraton is a page from the Diamond Sutra, *one of the most important Mahayana sacred texts. It shows the Buddha teaching his elderly follower, the monk Subhuti. This copy was made in China in 868 C.E.*

In Tibet, sacred words called mantras *are painted or carved in the Tibetan alphabet onto prayer stones.*

The Diamond Sutra

The *Diamond Sutra* is a short text of about three hundred verses, which forms part of a collection of texts called the *Sutras of Perfect Wisdom*. "Perfect Wisdom" means gaining a full and complete insight into how things really are. The *Diamond Sutra* was composed in about 300 C.E. and translated into Tibetan and Chinese. Its main teaching is that nothing exists by itself—everything is interconnected. This is why nothing in the world is fixed or everlasting. Like a diamond that is hard enough to cut through other materials, the *Diamond Sutra* is thought to have the power to cut through ignorance for those who study it carefully.

Tibetan Texts

The sacred texts of the Tibetan Buddhists are translations of Indian writings, collected between the seventh and fourteenth centuries C.E. The texts are divided into two sections—the *Kanjur* and the *Tenjur*. The Kanjur, or "Word of the Buddha," contains more than one thousand texts of the Buddha's teachings. The Tenjur, or "Treatises," contains some three thousand treatises and commentaries on the teachings. Another famous Tibetan text is the *Bardo Thodrol*, or *Tibetan Book of the Dead*. When a person is dying, a monk reads to them from this book. The words are intended to guide the person safely through Bardo, a world between death and rebirth.

Practice, Places of Worship, and Holy Days

Some Western Buddhists do not like to use the word "worship" to describe how they express their beliefs because they feel it implies worship of God or a god. They prefer "practice" instead, or puja, an Indian word for ritual or prayer. Buddhist practice varies around the world but usually includes honoring the Buddha at home or in the vihara and observing festivals and other holy days. For many Buddhists, this is a way of gaining "merit," which will help to ensure that their next lives are good ones. When they worship, they acknowledge what is most valuable in life and resolve to follow it. They believe this will lessen their suffering in this life as well as in possible future lives.

Visiting a Vihara

A *vihara* is a Buddhist temple or monastery. The earliest viharas were simple huts, built by the Buddha's first followers. The monks stayed in them during the rainy season when the weather made it difficult for them to travel. Buddhists may visit the vihara at any time, although many have specific times for puja, conducted by the monks. After entering the shrine room, Buddhists kneel and bow three times in front of the image of the Buddha installed there. The three bows represent the Buddha, the Dharma, and the Sangha. Then the worshipers repeat their commitment to the Three Jewels and recite the Five Moral Precepts (*see page 20*).

Offerings and Chanting

As part of Buddhist practice, people may place offerings of flowers, candles, and incense in front of the Buddha's image. Each offering has a special significance. Fresh flowers will eventually droop and die, a reminder that nothing lasts for ever. Candles light up a room just as the Buddha's teaching lights up people's lives. Like the Dharma, the sweet smell of incense spreads everywhere, reminding Buddhists that even their smallest actions have an effect. These offerings are accompanied by chanting.

Chanting is believed to be a means of calming and stilling the mind and a way of setting up a peaceful vibration, both within the body and by sending the sound out into the world. Chanting has been used through the ages to help practitioners memorize Buddhist texts. It is also often seen as an offering to the Buddha. Here's an example of a Buddhist chant:

"Offerings to the Buddha.
Reverencing the Buddha, we offer flowers—
Flowers that today are fresh and sweetly
  blooming,
Flowers that tomorrow are faded and fallen.

Our bodies too, like flowers, will pass away.

Reverencing the Buddha, we offer candles.
To him, who is the light, we offer light.
From his greater lamp a lesser lamp we light within us:
The lamp of bodhi shining within our hearts.

Reverencing the Buddha, we offer incense.
Incense whose fragrance pervades the air.
The fragrance of the perfect life, sweeter than incense,
Spreads in all directions throughout the world."

Children at a vihara in London, UK, show their respect for the Buddha by leaving offerings in front of his image.

In Our Own Words

"When we go to the temple, we have to get up earlier than usual. We take some food to offer the monks for their midday meal and to share with our other friends. We wear white because white is a symbol of purity. We bow three times in respect to the Buddha and the monks because we have so much to learn from them. Chanting in the ancient language of Pali makes me imagine Indian people of a thousand years ago doing exactly the same ceremony that we do today. When the ceremony is nearly finished, we do meditation, just for a few minutes. Afterwards we help offer the midday meal for the monks, and we sit together in a circle on the floor to share our lunch with the rest of the temple-goers."

Meditation

Meditation is central to Buddhist practice. Buddhists believe that through training their minds, they can overcome their ignorance, greed, and hatred and understand the true nature of things. The Buddha himself gained Enlightenment while meditating. Meditation is also linked to three steps on the Noble Eightfold Path—right effort, right mindfulness, and right concentration. Through meditation, a person can quiet or still the mind in order to experience inner peace. Learning to meditate, however, takes time, and it is important to have a good teacher. It is also important to find a suitable place and time. Many Buddhists meditate every day, on their own or in a group. There are many different kinds of meditation, but often Buddhists sit in a quiet room, eyes closed, and focus attention on their breath.

Places of Worship

Buddhist places of worship vary in style, depending on the country and particular Buddhist group. Traditionally, they are purpose-built for Buddhist practices, but in many Western countries Buddhists have converted old buildings into temples. The stupa provided the earliest focus of worship in Buddhism. After the death of the Buddha, his ashes were divided and placed in stupas in various parts of northern India. Today, these dome-shaped funeral mounds are found all over the Buddhist world, many containing the relics of great Buddhist teachers. They vary in shape from country to country; for example, in China and Japan most stupas are pagodas. When visiting a stupa, Buddhists may walk around it clockwise many times. As they walk, they may also chant *mantras*, or sacred verses, in honor of the Buddha and his teaching.

The striking white dome of the Swayambunath stupa in Kathmandu, Nepal. No one is sure exactly when the stupa was built, but by the thirteenth century it had become an important Buddhist center.

A Buddhist pilgrim at the Jokhang Temple in Lhasa, Tibet. He is standing next to a row of giant prayer wheels, which he spins as he passes in order to release the prayers.

Places of Pilgrimage

Many Buddhists like to make pilgrimages to sacred stupas, shrines, and places associated with the Buddha's life. For Tibetan Buddhists, the holiest site is the Jokhang Temple in Lhasa. Built in the seventh century C.E., legend has it that the temple stands on the site of a great underground lake in which people could see their future. On entering the temple, pilgrims pass rows of huge prayer wheels, or canisters that contain written prayers, which can be spun to dispense blessings on the world. Pilgrims can set the prayer wheels spinning as they make their way to the main hall, which contains an ancient bronze image of the Buddha sitting on top of a golden throne. The hall also contains shrines dedicated to Avalokiteshvara and other bodhisattvas, whose qualities pilgrims may contemplate in the calm environment of the temple. Outside the temple, the flagstones have been worn smooth by thousands of pilgrims prostrating themselves on the ground out of respect for the Buddha.

Art and Symbolism

Buddhist artists have created exquisite statues, paintings, and carvings. Buddhist art, however, is not simply decorative. Its purpose is to remind, support, and reinforce the Buddha's teachings. The earliest works were cave paintings and carvings, showing scenes from the Buddha's life. For hundreds of years after his death, the Buddha was not shown in person. Instead, he was represented by symbols, such as a bodhi tree (for Enlightenment), footprints (for his travels), or a wheel (for the Dharma). In scenes of his past lives, he was shown as a deer or other animal. The first images of the Buddha appeared by the first century C.E.

➤ *A modern image of the Buddha from a temple in Sri Lanka shows his long earlobes and tightly curled hair.*

Buddha Images

Buddhists do not actually worship images of the Buddha. The images represent the possibility of Enlightenment, the Buddha's teachings, and his special qualities, such as tranquility and compassion. They inspire Buddhists to remember these qualities and develop them within themselves. Images show a variety of ancient signs that mark the Buddha as an extraordinary human being. These include long earlobes, tightly curled hair, and lotus or wheel signs on the soles of his feet. In Mahayana Buddhism, there are also many images of bodhisattvas. They can be identified by the symbolic objects they carry, such as lotus flowers or diamond thunderbolts.

Mudras

In images of the Buddha and bodhisattvas, hands and fingers are portrayed being held in special symbolic gestures, called *mudras*. Mudra is a Sanskrit word meaning "sign" or "seal." In the *abhaya* (fearlessness) mudra, one hand is raised with its palm facing forward in a sign of protection and reassurance. In the *dharmachakra* (wheel-turning) mudra, both hands are held together to symbolize the teaching of the Dharma. The *dhyana* (meditation) mudra is a sign of meditation, with both hands resting in the lap. In the *bhumisparsha* (earth-touching) mudra, the Buddha touches the earth with one hand, just as he did at his Enlightenment (*see page* 9).

Mandalas

A mandala *is a circular, symbolic picture map showing the way to Enlightenment. It is used by Tibetan Buddhists to focus their minds for meditation. Around the outside is a protective ring of flames to burn away impurities such as greed, hatred, and ignorance. A second ring of thunderbolts shows the indestructible nature of Enlightenment. A final ring of lotus flowers symbolizes the purity of the land the meditating person is entering. Inside are four open gateways leading to the center. Here, there stands a picture of a bodhisattva representing a quality, such as wisdom or compassion. As a person meditates on the mandala, his or her mind moves through the different parts of the picture to reach the center of the mandala—Enlightenment, freedom from suffering.*

This mandala has been made from colored sand by Tibetan monks. The mandala will later be destroyed at a special ceremony, a reminder of the Buddha's teaching that nothing lasts for ever; all is transitory.

Buddhist Festivals

Many Buddhist festivals are celebrated during the year. The majority are associated with events from the Buddha's life, such as his birth, Enlightenment, and parinirvana; the lives of great Buddhist teachers; or major episodes in Buddhist history. Some are observed by Buddhists everywhere; others are special to particular groups. Celebrations vary from country to country and are influenced by local customs and traditions. Many festivals fall at the time of the full moon because, traditionally, this is when the key events in the Buddha's life are said to have happened. This is also when the monks traditionally met to recite the Dharma and rules of the monastic order (*see page 36*).

Wesak

For Theravada Buddhists and many others, the most important festival of the year is Wesak. It takes place on the full moon day of April or May and celebrates the Buddha's Enlightenment. Some Buddhists remember his birth and death on this day too. To mark Wesak, people may decorate their homes and viharas with lamps and candles that represent the light of Enlightenment. They may also visit the vihara for a special Wesak puja and to take gifts for the monks. Many Buddhists exchange Wesak cards, decorated with symbols such as lotus flowers or Dharma wheels.

The Sacred Tooth

A Theravada festival, Asala, occurs in July or August. It commemorates the first talk given by the Buddha after his Enlightenment. In Kandy, Sri Lanka, a series of spectacular processions, or *peraheras*, takes place through the streets. At the height of the festival, there is a parade of beautifully decorated elephants accompanied by dancers, drummers, and musicians. Carried on the back of one of the

A huge, illuminated Wesak decoration from Sri Lanka shows the chariot in which Siddhartha rode when he saw the Four Sights.

elephants is a replica of a golden casket. The original is kept safely in the nearby Temple of the Tooth. This temple contains a very precious relic, said to be one of the Buddha's own teeth.

▲ *Children in Japan dress up to celebrate the Hana Matsuri festival. They are wearing flowers in their hair to honor the Buddha.*

Hana Matsuri

The festival of Hana Matsuri is a very important one for Mahayana Buddhists in Japan. Celebrated in April, the festival marks the birth of the Buddha. It is also a flower festival, celebrating the coming of spring. (*Hana* is Japanese for flower; *matsuri* means festival.) At Hana Matsuri, model flower gardens are set up in the courtyards of Buddhist temples, as reminders of the garden in which the Buddha is believed to have been born. Images of the baby Buddha are placed in the gardens. Visitors pour spoonfuls of scented tea over the images, to remember the story of the scented water sent by the gods to bathe the Buddha at his birth.

In Our Own Words

"On the day of Wesak, I usually take the day off work. I spend some relaxing at home and the rest at the Buddhist Center with my friends. At the Center, some of us meditate together. In the evening, loads of people meet there, some of them with their children. We all bring vegetarian food for a big shared meal, and then we go up to the shrine hall. There's usually a talk about the meaning of the Buddha's Enlightenment, and then we have a special puja, or ritual, to celebrate his life and remind ourselves that we are trying to follow his example. There is lots of chanting and readings and people light candles and incense in front of the Buddha figure. The small children play and run up and down the corridor when they get bored!"

4 Monks and Monasteries

The Buddha spent a large part of his life living as a wandering holy man and teaching the Dharma. Following in his footsteps, some devout Buddhists leave their homes and belongings and dedicate their lives to learning and practicing the Buddha's teachings. They form the monastic Sangha, or community, of monks (bhikkhus) and nuns (bhikkhunis).

Becoming a Monk

In many Theravada countries, young boys spend several months in a monastery as part of their education. Some then leave and return to their families and the outside world. Others stay on in the monastery and are ordained as monks. In Sri Lanka, the ordination ceremony dates back to the time of the Buddha. First, the young monk has his head and beard shaved as a sign that he is no longer living an everyday life. Then he bathes as a symbol of his desire to live a purer life. He kneels in front of the senior monk present and asks permission to wear his yellow

Boys in Sri Lanka being ordained as Buddhist monks. They are kneeling in front of the senior monks and holding their new robes.

monk's robes and to be ordained. (In Tibet and Myanmar, monks' robes are maroon. In Japan, they are black.) He also begs forgiveness for his faults and pledges his commitment to the Three Jewels. If the monks consider him suitable, he is accepted as a bhikkhu.

The Eight Requisites

To be detached from worldly ties (since attachment brings suffering), Buddhist monks and nuns have very few personal possessions. Traditionally, since the Buddha's time, they have only been allowed to own eight items that are absolutely necessary, called the Eight Requisites. These are three robes, an alms bowl, a belt, a water-strainer, a walking stick, a toothpick, a needle, and a razor (for monks). All else belongs to the monastery.

Western Orders

The Friends of the Western Buddhist Order is one of the best-known new Buddhist groups in Western countries (*see page 44*). Women and men who join the Order itself make a serious commitment to the Dharma, but they do not become nuns or monks. They do not live in monasteries or rely on the local community for food, as monks traditionally do in many Buddhist countries. Some teach and run Buddhist centers. Others have ordinary jobs or work in businesses which promote "right livelihood" (*see page 17*), such as running bookshops that sell books about Buddhism. Similarly, Shambala International has many Buddhist retreat centers in North America, including four in the U.S., and a monastic center on Cape Breton Island, Nova Scotia, Canada. There are Buddhist centers and practicing communities in many U.S. cities.

These women are being ordained as Buddhist nuns in Britain in a monastery that follows the Theravada tradition.

Rules for Monks and Nuns

Monks and nuns must follow strict rules of discipline, called the *vinaya*, set down by the Buddha. The vinaya is one of the three baskets of the Tipitaka (*see page 23*). It sets out the rules, then explains when and in what circumstances they were devised and gives examples. Many monasteries have 227 rules, but the number can vary in some Mahayana groups. These rules include the Ten Moral Precepts, which are the Five Moral Precepts followed by lay Buddhists (*see page 20*) plus five other rules: not eating after midday, not singing or dancing in a frivolous way, not wearing jewelry or perfume, not sleeping on a soft bed, and not accepting gifts of money.

Life in the Monastery

Monks and nuns live a very simple lifestyle. Typically, monks in a Theravada monastery get up early and have two meals—breakfast and lunch. After midday, they are only allowed water or tea. The monks' food is provided by local people who bring it to the monastery or invite the monks to their homes. During the day, time is set aside for meditation, studying the sacred texts, and conducting ceremonies and puja for laypeople. Traditionally, monks are also expected to teach, guide, and counsel anyone who wishes to learn about the Dharma or seeks their advice.

In a Zen monastery, life is very strict and strenuous. At the heart of the monastery is the *Zendo* or meditation hall, where the monks meditate and where they sleep on mats on the floor. Their few possessions are kept in a small locker. They take their simple meals in silence, after special chanting in which all the monks join. During the day, the monks spend long hours in the *Sodo*, or monastery school, studying under their *roshis* (masters).

Monks in the Jokhang Temple in Lhasa, Tibet, read from the sacred texts. Studying the sacred texts is an important part of their daily lives.

▲ *Zen monks in a monastery in Japan, practicing meditation. They spend many hours each day learning to meditate.*

In Our Own Words

"I am a fully ordained nun in the Karma Kagyu tradition of Tibetan Buddhism. There were two reasons why I felt I wanted to take this commitment for the rest of my life. The first was emotional: I had an overwhelming feeling that this was the only thing I wanted to do. Less immediate, but still relevant, was the rational understanding that becoming ordained was the best way to make life meaningful and to become more useful to others. This understanding built up gradually over several years, nurtured by the advice and good example of Tibetan lama-monks as well as a few Western monks and nuns. That was over fifteen years ago, and I have never regretted it. Life just gets better and better!"

5 Buddhism and Society

In traditional Buddhist countries, such as Sri Lanka and Thailand, the Sangha has played, and continues to play, a very important role in society. Viharas and temples are often at the center of village or town life and are used as schools and community centers. While lay Buddhists have a duty to support their local monastery and its monks, the monks teach people about the Dharma and help them to live life according to Buddhist principles.

Moral Issues

For Buddhists, all moral issues are to be approached with the Five Moral Precepts and the teachings on wisdom, compassion, loving kindness, and karma in mind. Although there are guidelines for how people should behave, it is up to each individual person to take responsibility for deciding what is right and wrong. The desire to achieve Enlightenment helps guide Buddhists to act morally.

Animal Welfare

The first of the Five Precepts is to undertake to avoid killing or harming any living thing and, on the positive side, to cultivate loving-kindness. Many Buddhists try to develop a loving appreciation for animals and nature, as well as other people. The Buddha taught that if people are training themselves to become more loving and kind, they need to use imagination. If they remember how it feels to suffer pain and fear, they will not wish to cause pain for others. The Buddha also taught that everything is dependent on other things, so all actions have consequences for the person doing them and for other living things. (For example, when poison is used to kill slugs, it also kills the birds that eat slugs.) This teaching has led some Buddhists to become deeply involved with environmental and ecological concerns.

In Asia, elephants such as this one have traditionally been used in the timber industry to haul logs from place to place.

In Myanmar, for example, Buddhists and conservationists are working together to protect the country's endangered elephants. Elephants have been used in Asia for centuries for work, war, ceremonial, and religious purposes. They often appear in Buddhist stories, such as the *Jatakas* (*see page 22*), as symbols of wisdom and strength. Today, Myanmar's elephants are seriously threatened by habitat loss and poaching. Human expansion in the area has brought the elephants and local people increasingly into conflict. In an innovative ecology project, Buddhists are helping conservationists collect vital information about the elephants. Monks are also working with local people in many places to help them live in harmony with the elephants and protect them.

Vegetarianism

To follow the First Precept, many Buddhists choose to be vegetarians. They do not eat meat because this involves killing a living thing. The Buddhist teachings do not, however, forbid people to eat meat, and in some countries, for example, in mountainous Tibet (where vegetation is scarce), meat is an important part of people's diets. Monks are expected to be grateful for whatever food people give them, including meat.

Monks receive gifts of food in Bangkok, Thailand. Local people hope to gain spiritual merit by giving food as alms. In return, the monks are grateful for whatever is put in their begging bowls. The monks take the food back to the monastery to eat.

Engaged Buddhism

Apart from conservation, many Buddhists are becoming involved in what they call "engaged Buddhism." This means becoming more "engaged," or active, in social work in such ways as setting up hospitals, hospices, and AIDS charities; in human rights, for example, by visiting prisoners; and in peace campaigning and politics (*see page 42*). Although "engaged Buddhism" represents a new and sometimes controversial chapter in Buddhism's history, it is nonetheless rooted in ancient Buddhist teachings of mindfulness, compassion, and loving kindness for all living beings.

A Tibetan monk and former political prisoner, Palden Gyatsu, leads a protest against British involvement in the international arms trade outside an arms fair in the UK in 1997.

International Network

The International Network of Engaged Buddhists (INEB) began in 1989 in Thailand. Since then, it has grown rapidly and now has members and runs projects in thirty-three countries. Its goal is to combine Buddhist spiritual practice with social action for a just and peaceful world. Non-Buddhists can join the INEB. They must simply be committed to helping others out of compassion, as in the INEB's 2005 visits to tsunami refugee camps. Another key INEB activity is helping war-torn areas resolve conflicts without using violence. For example, they have organized four annual Dharma Peace Walks in Cambodia.

Drug Rehabilitation

One example of "engaged Buddhism" in action is the work of the Wat Tham Krabok mountain monastery in Thailand. For the last fifty years, it has run a detoxification program for drug addicts, based on Buddhist principles. Addicts mostly come from Thailand but also from Europe and Australia. On arrival, they must take an oath stating their commitment to the program and to staying drug- and alcohol-free for the rest of their lives. The program itself is strict but highly successful. It involves drinking a special herbal mixture and taking herbal steam baths to get rid of toxins and cleanse the body. Monks and nuns are constantly on hand to supervise and to offer counseling and support.

Prison Visiting

The Angulimala Buddhist Prison Chaplaincy Organisation was set up in Britain in 1985 by an English Buddhist monk, Venerable Khemadhammo Mahathera. The organization is named after Angulimala, a notorious robber and murderer who was converted by the Buddha and became a monk. The story of Angulimala shows the principle on which the organization is based—that Enlightenment is possible in the most difficult circumstances and that people can change. A team of Buddhist chaplains visits prisons to teach inmates about Buddhism, although prisoners do not have to be or become Buddhists. The organization also holds training sessions for Buddhist chaplains who want to serve prisons.

Young drug addicts take part in a Buddhist ceremony in the Wat Tham Krabok monastery in Thailand.

6 Current Issues and World Role

As it moves into the twenty-first century, Buddhism faces many challenges. For many traditional Buddhist countries, the twentieth century proved a time of mixed fortunes. In countries such as China, Tibet, and Myanmar, Buddhists faced and continue to face persecution under the Communist and military regimes. For example, Buddhist monks such as Tenzin Delek Rinpoche have been imprisoned for life and must rely on international human rights groups to save them from the death penalty in China. In other Asian countries, war, ethnic conflict, and nationalist unrest put Buddhism under serious threat. As more countries have become Westernized and concerned with material wealth, the traditional values and teachings of Buddhism have sometimes been undermined. Nevertheless, in some places, such as Indonesia and India, Buddhism has begun to re-establish its presence and win new support. Meanwhile, it continues to expand quickly in the "new" territories of Europe, Australia, and North America.

The Dalai Lama, Tenzin Gyatso, leader of Tibet's Buddhists, now lives in exile in Dharamsala, India. His title means "a teacher whose wisdom is as deep as the ocean."

Buddhism in Exile

In 1951, Chinese Communists invaded Tibet. Until that time, the Dalai Lama had been Tibet's religious leader and head of its government. The Communist regime, however, objected to all religious practices. Hundreds of Buddhist monasteries were destroyed, thousands of monks imprisoned or killed, and the teaching and study of Buddhism was outlawed. In 1959, after an unsuccessful Tibetan uprising against the Chinese, the Dalai Lama fled to India where he now leads the Tibetans in exile. Many other monks and teachers also escaped, and they established a thriving Buddhist community in Dharamsala, India. Famous for his warmth, wisdom, and compassion, and believed by Tibetans to be a living bodhisattva, the Dalai Lama travels all over the world campaigning for the rights of the Tibetan people and suggesting nonviolent solutions to his country's problems. In 1989, he was awarded the Nobel Peace Prize.

Buddhism in India

By the twelfth century C.E., Buddhism had almost disappeared from India, and Hinduism and Islam became the country's major religions. Recently, however, Buddhism has enjoyed something of a revival in India, largely through the work of an Indian lawyer and politician, Dr. B. R. Ambedkar (1891–1956). Born into a *Dalit* family, Ambedkar spent his life fighting for equal rights for Dalits ("untouchables"), the lowest group, or caste, in Indian Hindu society. Hostility from orthodox Hindus towards Ambedkar's demands for social equality led him to break away from Hinduism. In 1956, just before his death, he became a Buddhist and committed himself to the Buddhist principle of equality. Millions of Dalits followed his lead, and the Ambedkar Buddhists have since become the largest single group of Buddhists in India.

▼ *Dr. Ambedkar addresses a large crowd in India before a mass conversion to Buddhism in 1956.*

Buddhism in the West

Buddhism reached the West at the end of the nineteenth century through the writings of Western scholars and their translations of Buddhist sacred texts. In 1881, the Pali Text Society was founded by a British scholar, T.W. Rhys Davids, while working for the Civil Service in Sri Lanka (then Ceylon). The Society collected, translated, and published the sacred texts of Theravada Buddhism and made them available in Britain. At the same time, people from traditionally Buddhist countries in Asia began to settle in Europe and North America. Later, Westerners became interested and began to convert to Buddhism.

Friends of the Western Buddhist Order

The Friends of the Western Buddhist Order was started by an English Buddhist monk, Venerable Sangharakshita. He had studied many different branches of Buddhism and wanted to form a Buddhist movement that combined elements of many traditions. He also wanted the movement to be suited to Western society. For example, order members do not wear robes but have a *kesa* (scarf) for special ceremonies. Highly committed Buddhists are ordained as "members" and take a new Buddhist name but do not become monks or nuns. The Order is based in the United Kingdom.

New Buddhist Movements

One of the fastest-growing of the new Buddhist groups in the West has been the Soka Gakkai, or "Society for the Creation of Value." It was founded in 1930 as an offshoot of the Nichiren school, based on the teachings of the Japanese monk, Nichiren (1222–1283). It teaches chanting (or singing Buddhist texts and mantras) as a means of achieving not only spiritual rewards but also health, personal happiness, and material gain. It set up centers in the United States in the 1960s and in Europe in the 1970s and 1980s. One of the main goals of Soka Gakkai is to build "a culture of peace," a positive step to help the war-torn world of today.

A member of the Western Buddhist Order honors the Buddha in a temple in Manchester, UK. He is wearing a kesa *(scarf) around his neck.*

In Our Own Words

The Future of Western Buddhism

"I think Buddhism will continue growing in the West. Buddhism emphasizes loving-kindness and says that each of us can change our own lives and the world by taking responsibility for the consequences of our actions. As people find greed more and more destructive to society and the environment, they may find Buddhism a very attractive and effective path.

We will continue to see three particular features in Western Buddhism:

1. *Women will be taken much more seriously than they have been traditionally.*
2. *The relationship between the monastic and lay Buddhist communities will change because Western laypeople are well-educated and may study, meditate, and teach as much as monks or nuns.*
3. *Western Buddhists will become even more socially and politically active."*

▼ *A Buddhist temple in Little Tokyo, Los Angeles. In the twenty-first century, Buddhism is set to become more popular in countries beyond its original Asian homeland.*

Glossary

anatta (Sanskrit: *anatman*) the Pali word for no fixed self. Buddhists do not believe in a fixed soul or spirit that lives on after the body dies. They believe that everything is always changing.

anicca (Sanskrit: *anitya*) the Pali word for the Buddhist belief in impermanence: Nothing lasts forever but is always changing.

arahat (Sanskrit: *arhat*) the Pali word for an Enlightened person who is on the highest stage leading to nirvana and whose mind is free from hatred, ignorance, and greed

bhikkhu (Sanskrit: *bhikshu*) the Pali word for a Buddhist monk

bhikkhuni (Sanskrit: *bhikshuni*) the Pali word for a Buddhist nun

bodhi tree the fig tree under which the Buddha is believed to have gained Enlightenment

bodhisattva a heroic figure in Mahayana Buddhism who is believed to have gained Enlightenment and become a Buddha. Out of compassion for the world, the bodhisattva chooses to help other people overcome their suffering.

caste the classes or divisions in Hindu society

Dalits members of the lowest rank of Hindu society, previously known as "untouchables." The word Dalit means "oppressed."

Dharma (Pali: *Dhamma*) the Pali word for the Buddha's teaching

dukkha (Sanskrit: *duhka*) the Pali word for suffering

enlightenment the experience of understanding the truth about the world and how things really are

karma (Pali: *kamma*) the Sanskrit word for the good and bad actions that affect a person's position in this and future lives

kesa a scarf worn by members of the Friends of the Western Buddhist Order for special ceremonies

Mahayana one of the two main schools of Buddhism. It means "the great way."

mandala a circular picture that Tibetan Buddhists use to help them meditate. In their minds, they follow a path into the center of the picture as if following a map.

meditation a central part of Buddhist practice. The goal of meditation is to quiet or still the mind in order to experience inner peace.

metta (Sanskrit: *maitri*) the Pali word for the key Buddhist virtue of loving-kindness and generosity to others, without thought of reward

Mogul the Muslim rulers of India from 1526–1857

mudra (Pali: *mudda*) the Sanskrit word for symbolic positions of the hands, seen in images of the Buddha and bodhisattvas. Each mudra has a special meaning.

nirvana (Pali: *nibbana*) the perfect peace and happiness entered when the cycle of birth and rebirth is broken and suffering ends

pagoda a style of stupa or temple found in China, Japan, and parts of Southeast Asia

Pali an ancient Indian language in which the texts of the Theravada Buddhists were first written down

parinirvana (Pali: *parinibbana*) the Sanskrit word for the final and complete nirvana reached when the Buddha passed away

puja the name given to a ceremony of devotion and worship in Buddhism and Hinduism

Sangha the community of Buddhists, which began with the Buddha's first followers. For some Buddhists, the sangha particularly means monks and nuns; for others, it includes all Buddhists.

Sanskrit an ancient Indian language in which many Mahayana sacred texts are written down. It is a sacred language for Hindus.

Silk Road an ancient overland route between Europe and Asia, along which goods such as silk were carried. Later, ideas and religions spread along this path as well.

skandha (Pali: *khandha*) the Sanskrit word for each of the five parts or elements that are believed to make up a human being. Buddhists believe that the way these five parts come together changes with each rebirth.

stupa a dome-shaped Buddhist monument

sutra (Pali: *sutta*) the Sanskrit word for a short Buddhist sacred text

Tantric a form of Buddhism from Tibet, based on mysterious texts describing rituals, magic, and meditation techniques

Theravada one of the two main schools of Buddhism. It means "way of the elders."

Tipitaka (Sanskrit: *Tripitaka*) the Pali word for the sacred texts of the Theravada Buddhists, also known as the *Pali Canon*

vihara a Buddhist monastery or temple

vinaya the rules of discipline for Buddhist monks and nuns

Zen a school of Mahayana Buddhism from China and Japan. The word Zen means "meditation."

Time Line

c. 623 B.C.E.	Siddhartha Gautama born in Lumbini, Nepal
c. 588 B.C.E.	Siddhartha gains Enlightenment in Bodh Gaya, India, and becomes the Buddha
c. 543 B.C.E.	The Buddha passes away in Kushinagara, India
c. 543–443 B.C.E.	Two councils held to collect the Buddha's teachings together. Buddhism splits into the Theravada and Mahayana schools
268–239 B.C.E.	Reign of Emperor Ashoka Maurya in India. Buddhism becomes the major faith of India
c. 250 B.C.E.	Buddhism reaches Sri Lanka and, later, Myanmar
1st century B.C.E.	*Tipitaka* (*Pali Canon*) written down
1st century C.E.	Buddhism reaches China. First images of the Buddha are made
4th century C.E.	Buddhism reaches Korea
7th century C.E.	Buddhism reaches Tibet
6th century C.E.	Buddhism reaches Japan
12th century C.E.	Buddhism almost disappears from India. Zen Buddhism reaches Japan from China
13th century C.E.	Buddhism becomes the official religion in Thailand, Cambodia, and Laos
1881	Pali Text Society founded to translate Pali texts into English
1891	Mahabodhi Society founded in Sri Lanka to unite Buddhists and raise funds to restore sacred Buddhist sites in India
1907	First Buddhist Society in Britain formed
1930	Buddhist Society of America formed in the United States
1935	The present Dalai Lama, beleived to be a bodhisattva, born in Tibet
1956	In India, Dr Ambedkar converts many people to Buddhism
1967	Friends of the Western Buddhist Order founded in the UK
1989	Dalai Lama receives the Nobel Peace Prize
1989	International Network of Engaged Buddhists begins in Thailand
2005	China spares Tibetan Monk Tenzin Delek Rinpoche from unfair death sentence, bowing to pressure from international human rights groups

Books

Demi. *Buddha.* Henry Holt and Company, 1996.

Ladner, Lorne. *The Wheel of Great Compassion.* Wisdom Publications, 2001.

Marchant, Kerena *The Buddha and Buddhism.* Great Religious Leaders. (series). Smart Apple Media, 2002.

Wilkinson, Philip. *Buddhism.* Eyewitness Books (series). DK Publishing Inc., 2003.

Winston, Diana. *Wide Awake: A Buddhist Guide for Teens.* Penguin USA, 2003.

Metcalf, Franz and Monk Song Yoon. *Buddha in Your Backpack: Everyday Buddhism for Teens.* Seastone, 2002.

Web Sites

tibet.dharmakara.net/TibCulture.html

www.dharma-haven.org/tibetan/meaning-of-om-mani-padme-hung.htm

www.dzogchen.org/teachings/faq.htm

www.japan-guide.com/e/e2055.html

www.omniglot.com/writing/tibetan.htm

www.sgi-usa.org/thesgiusa/index.html

www.studentsforafreetibet.org/

www.thaistudents.com/buddha/

Index